X-TREME FACTS: U.S. HISTORY

MONUMENTS AND MEMORIALS

by Marcia Abramson

BEARPORT PUBLISHING

Minneapolis, Minnesota

Credits:
© Cover, clockwise from bottom left, Martin Gardeazabal/Shutterstock; Hugo Brizard-YouGoPhoto/Shutterstock; Erika Cross/Shutterstock; Andrey_Kuzmin/Shutterstock; Title Page, 8, 11 top, Muddymari/Shutterstock.com; 4 top, Chief Photographer's Mate Johnny Bivera/ Public Domain; 4, monkographic/Shutterstock; 5 top, United States Geological Survey/Public Domain; 5 bottom, GaudiLab/Shutterstock; 6, ChameleonsEye/Shutterstock.com; 7 left, andersphoto/Shutterstock; 7 top right, Skreidzeleu/Shutterstock.com; 7 right, Vyntage Visuals/Shutterstock; 9, DiegoMariottini/Shutterstock.com; 9 bottom right, Kabardins photo/Shutterstock; 9 top right, Gilbert Stuart/ Public Domain; 9 top left, Natalia Yurkova/Shutterstock; 10 left, Dima Moroz/Shutterstock.com; 10, Orhan Cam/Shutterstock.com; 11 left, Wknight94/Creative Commons; 11 middle, Paul Michael Hughes/Shutterstock; 11 right, Library of Congress/Public Domain; 12, U.S. National Archives and Records Administration/Public Domain; 12 right, Public Domain; 13 top left, Pigprox/Shutterstock.com; 13 bottom left, National Archives and Records Administration Records of the U.S/Public Domain; 13 bottom middle, DeMarsico, Dick/New York World-Telegram and the Sun Newspaper Photograph Collection (Library of Congress); 13 bottom right, John Trumbull/Public Domain; 14, National Park Service/Public Domain; 14 top right, Ser Amantio di Nicolao/Creative Commons; 15 top, Public Domain; 15 top right, Women of Protest: Photographs from the Records of the National Woman's Party, Manuscript Division, Library of Congress, Washington, D.C./ Public Domain; 15 bottom right, Library of Congress's Prints and Photographs division/Public Domain; 15 bottom right, Public Domain; 15 left, Gilbert Stuart/Public Domain; 16 bottom, Frontpage/Shutterstock; 16 top, Everett Historical/Shutterstock; 17 top left, Dawalker61/ Creative Commons; 17 bottom, John Brueske/Shutterstock; 17 top right, Jess Kraft/Shutterstock;17 top middle, jaroslava V/Shutterstock; 17 bottom middle, Everett Collection/Shutterstock; 18 bottom, 19 left, Lucky-photographer/Shutterstock; 18 right, Happy Together/ Shutterstock; 19 top, New York World-Telegram and the Sun Newspaper Photograph Collection (Library of Congress)/Public Domain; 19 bottom right, Ramakrishna Gundra/Creative Commons; 19 bottom, Dimitris Leonidas/Shutterstock; 19 middle, Luciano Mortula - LGM/ Shutterstock; 20, John De Winter/Shutterstock; 21 top left, NPS/Public Domain; 21 middle left, Joshua Avramson; 21 bottom left, irin-k/ Shutterstock; 21 right, Tinasuzanne/Creative Commons; 22, Roller Coaster Philosophy/Creative Commons; 22 right, Public Domain; 23 top, Public Domain; 23 bottom, Jules Tavernier and Paul Frenzeny/Public Domain; 24, U.S. National Park Service/Public Domain; 25 top, US Army Photo/Public Domain; 25 bottom, Public Domain; 26 bottom left, National Archives and Records Administration/Public Domain; 26 top right, U.S. Navy/Public Domain; 26, U.S. Navy/Public Domain; 27 top, U.S. National Park Service/Public Domain; 27 middle right, Ron Elias/Northrop Grumman/U.S. National Park Service/Public Domain; 27 bottom left, Pacific Historic Parks/Public Domain; 27, Pacific Historic Parks/Public Domain; 28, Markuskun/Public Domain; 29 bottom left, Dick DeMarsico, World Telegram staff photographer/Public Domain; 28-29, Austen Photography

Developed and produced for Bearport Publishing by BlueAppleWorks Inc.
Managing Editor for BlueAppleWorks: Melissa McClellan
Art Director: T.J. Choleva
Photo Research: Jane Reid
Editor: Jane Yates

Library of Congress Cataloging-in-Publication Data

Names: Abramson, Marcia, 1949– author.
Title: Monuments and memorials / by Marcia Abramson.
Description: Minneapolis, Minnesota : Bearport Publishing Company, [2021] | Series: Xtreme facts: U.S. history | Includes bibliographical references and index.
Identifiers: LCCN 2020012913 (print) | LCCN 2020012914 (ebook) | ISBN 9781647471194 (library binding) | ISBN 9781647471262 (paperback) | ISBN 9781647471330 (ebook)
Subjects: LCSH: National monuments—United States—Juvenile literature. | Memorials—United States—Juvenile literature.
Classification: LCC E159 .A27 2021 (print) | LCC E159 (ebook) | DDC 363.6/8—dc23
LC record available at https://lccn.loc.gov/2020012913
LC ebook record available at https://lccn.loc.gov/2020012914

For more information, write to Bearport Publishing, 5357 Penn Avenue South, Minneapolis, MN 55419.
Printed in the United States of America.

Contents

MONUMENT OR MEMORIAL

Is There a Difference?

What are monuments? How about memorials? And what's the difference? Both monuments and memorials are designed to **commemorate** something or someone important, usually a famous person or a big event. Some say memorials more often honor the death of a historic figure or a tragic event. But most people use the two words to mean the same thing. For example, the Washington Monument is classified as a memorial, not a monument! So, is there a difference? Kind of, but not really.

Arizona and California are tied for the most national monuments with 18 each!

Washington, D.C., has the most national memorials—11 of them.

The United States has 128 national monuments and 30 national memorials.

Mount St. Helens National Volcanic Monument in Washington State was created after an eruption there killed 57 people in 1980.

It cost more than $100 million each to build the memorials honoring World War II **veterans** and Dr. Martin Luther King, Jr.

United States presidents get to choose new national monuments and memorials.

A WELCOMING LADY

The Statue of Liberty

In 1886, the Statue of Liberty was completed on a small island in New York Harbor. During the second half of the nineteenth century, the Statue of Liberty became a **symbol** of immigration. The figure was the first landmark **immigrants** saw when they arrived to the country by ship. The monument represents the United States' welcoming embrace of all people.

The Statue of Liberty National Monument also includes nearby Ellis Island. Over 12 million immigrants came through Ellis Island from 1892 to 1954.

The Statue of Liberty was a gift from France for America's 100th birthday in 1876.

The Statue of Liberty monument is as **tall as a 22-story building!**

Lightning strikes the statue about **600 times a year.**

The statue weighs 450,000 pounds (204,117 kg). That's **heavier than 100 hippos!**

French workers shipped the copper statue to New York in 350 pieces. Luckily, they also sent instructions!

TALLEST IN D.C.

The Washington Monument

The Washington Monument is a double first! It honors the first U.S. president, George Washington, and it was the first national memorial in Washington, D.C. When it opened on February 21, 1885, the Washington Monument was the tallest building in the world. The stunning structure is 555 feet (169 m) tall. It sits in a park that lies between the U.S. Capitol and the Lincoln Memorial. This part of Washington, D.C., with its monuments, memorials, and museums, is known as the National Mall.

There is no cement holding the Washington Monument together!

The Lincoln Memorial, Washington Monument, and U.S. Capitol all line up in the National Mall.

The Washington Monument remained the world's tallest building until 1889, when the Eiffel Tower was completed in Paris, France.

Visitors can see more than 30 miles (48 km) in every direction from the top of the memorial.

The monument is not all the same color! Construction was interrupted for a few years. When the work began again, a slightly different color of marble was used. The line separating the two colors of marble is clearly visible.

President George Washington never lived in Washington, D.C. The city was still being built when he died in 1799!

The 50 American flags around the memorial symbolize the 50 states.

REMEMBERING ABE

The Lincoln Memorial

As president, Abraham Lincoln dedicated his life to serving and preserving the country he loved. The giant Lincoln Memorial is a fitting tribute to this giant of a man. A 19-ft (5.8-m) tall statue of the 16th president sits at the memorial's center. Lincoln's left hand is clenched to symbolize his strength and desire to keep the country together. His right hand is open, showing his softer, caring side.

The memorial was modeled after a Greek temple because **democracy was born in ancient Athens.**

The memorial has 36 columns, one for each state in the country at the time of Lincoln's death.

The stone used to build the Lincoln Memorial came from six states across the country.

Six brothers did most of the stonecutting for Lincoln's statue.

Construction on the memorial began on Lincoln's birthday, February 12, 1914. It took eight years to complete.

Lincoln's statue is made of white marble from Georgia.

There's a mistake on the wall of the memorial! The mistake was fixed, but visitors can still spot the "F" that used to be an "E."

HOPE CARVED IN STONE

The Martin Luther King, Jr. National Memorial

In 1963, Dr. Martin Luther King, Jr. gave his most famous speech at the Lincoln Memorial during the March on Washington. He shared his dream of a future America that would provide all of its citizens with freedom, equality, and justice. Forty-eight years later, his own memorial was dedicated in nearby West Potomac Park. Dr. King, who was killed in 1968, is the first African American with a memorial on or near the National Mall.

More than **250,000 people** attended the March on Washington, which was a protest against racial inequality.

Dr. King believed that protests should always be peaceful.

A 450 ft (137 m) wall surrounds the statue of Dr. King. The wall is covered with quotes from his speeches, sermons, and writings.

Dr. King skipped 9th and 12th grades and went to **Morehouse College when he was just 15!**

Dr. King was a leader of the Montgomery bus **boycott** that began when **Rosa Parks was arrested for refusing to give up her bus seat to a white passenger.**

Only two Americans have national holidays in honor of their birthdays. One is George Washington and the other is Dr. King.

A HOME FOR EQUALITY

The Belmont-Paul Women's Equality National Monument

The Belmont-Paul Women's Equality National Monument looks like just an ordinary townhouse—but what a history it has! Located just around the corner from the Capitol, the home is one of the oldest in Washington, D.C. But that's not the reason this building is famous. In 1929, it became the headquarters of the National Woman's Party (NWP), a group fighting for women's rights. The home is named for two of the party's leaders, Alice Paul and Alva Belmont.

Women did not have the right to vote in U.S. elections **until 1920**.

The monument includes a museum that focuses on the women's suffrage movement.

In 1923, **the NWP introduced the Equal Rights Amendment, which would make it illegal to treat men and women differently.** Almost 100 years later, it still has not become law.

In 1917, Alice Paul (*right*) led 2,000 women in protests outside the White House. They wanted to pressure President Woodrow Wilson into supporting women's right to vote.

Future First Lady Abigail Adams was an early supporter of women's rights. She asked her husband, John Adams, to "remember the ladies" in the Declaration of Independence.

Abolitionist Sojourner Truth campaigned for suffrage for all, including African Americans and women.

PRESIDENTIAL MOUNTAIN

Mount Rushmore National Memorial

In 1923, the people of South Dakota started looking for a way to attract tourists to their great state. In 1925, sculptor Gutzon Borglum had an idea. He began carving the faces of four presidents into the side of Mount Rushmore—George Washington, Thomas Jefferson, Abraham Lincoln, and Theodore Roosevelt. He used a lot of dynamite to blast and shape the stone—about 450,000 tons (400,000 MT)! Amazingly, no one was killed during the 14 years of construction.

First Lady Eleanor Roosevelt asked that suffragist Susan B. Anthony appear on the mountain, but she was turned down.

The four presidents were chosen to represent different parts of the nation's history. Washington represented its birth, Jefferson its growth, Lincoln its preservation, and Roosevelt its development.

Nearby, **a giant memorial** to Crazy Horse, a Lakota leader, is being carved to honor Native American peoples.

Each head is about 60 ft (18 m) tall. That's about **the size of three giraffes standing on one another.**

Mount Rushmore will last a long time. The sculpture's rate of **erosion** is estimated at only 1 inch (2.5 cm) every 10,000 years!

Some of the first people to see Mount Rushmore thought Thomas Jefferson was Martha Washington!

A GROWING MONUMENT

Giant Sequoia National Monument

Many of the world's oldest and biggest trees live in the Sequoia National Forest and Giant Sequoia National Monument in California. Giant sequoias are the fastest-growing trees and can live for more than 3,000 years. One of them, the General Sherman, is considered the world's largest living thing. It is 275 ft (83 m) tall and over 36 ft (11 m) in diameter at the base.

A sequoia can shoot up by as much as **4 ft (1.2 m) per year.**

Sequoias can have branches up to 7 ft (2.1 m) in diameter. Their bark can grow 2 ft (0.6 m) thick in places.

President Theodore Roosevelt was inspired to create national parks and forests after sleeping under giant sequoias.

A fully grown sequoia rises more than 250 ft (76 m) into the sky. That's taller than the Statue of Liberty.

In 1881, a tunnel was cut through a sequoia called the Wawona Tree. The weakened tree died in 1969.

The base of a sequoia tree can be as wide **as the length of two pickup trucks parked bumper-to-bumper.**

REACHING TO THE SKY

Devils Tower National Monument

Devils Tower, in northeastern Wyoming, became the first national monument in 1905. Most geologists think it formed when underground **magma** pushed up into the **sedimentary** rock on the surface. The tower is covered in hundreds of cracks and columns that make it a perfect spot for rock climbers. The monument is sacred to numerous Native American tribes who hold ceremonies at the top of Devils Tower.

Devils Tower got its English name after a translator made a mistake. He thought Native Americans called it Bad God's Tower.

The real Native American names for the formation include Bear Lodge, Tree Rock, Great Gray Horn, and Ghost Mountain.

Devils Tower is 867 ft (265 m) tall. That's more than twice as tall as the Statue of Liberty.

The top of Devils Tower is **big enough to hold a football field.**

Aliens landed at Devils Tower in the 1977 film *Close Encounters of the Third Kind.*

The National Park Service warns climbers to watch out for snakes, poison ivy, falcons, **wasps,** and falling rocks.

A CASTLE IN A CLIFF

Montezuma Castle National Monument

Montezuma Castle in Camp Verde, Arizona, is an old Native American cliff dwelling. Between 1100 and 1425, a group now known as the Sinagua built the five-story structure out of stone, timber, and **mortar**. No one knows why they built the castle so high on a cliff. Equally mysterious is why the Sinagua **abandoned** the site and migrated elsewhere.

Montezuma's Castle has more than 20 rooms and more floor space than 13 football fields!

The name Montezuma Castle is all wrong. The Aztec ruler Montezuma was born 40 years after the Sinagua abandoned the site . . .

. . . **The Montezuma Castle was** also more of **an apartment building** where many people lived rather than a castle!

Today, visitors can't enter the dwelling because it is fragile. Instead, they can see a display of how the Sinagua lived.

Modern **Hopi and Zuni** peoples are **descendents** of the Sinaguas.

Cliff dwellers climbed ladders to get to their homes. If enemies came, they could simply pull up the ladders!

PROTECTING A NATION

Fort Monroe National Monument

A fort has been guarding the southern tip of the Virginia Peninsula for more than 400 years! Colonists started building Fort Algernourne there in 1609. Fort Monroe, still standing today, was completed in 1834. This six-sided structure is the largest stone fort ever built in the United States. Fort Monroe was an active U.S. Army base until 2011, when it became a national monument.

In 1619, a Dutch ship landed near the fort, carrying the first enslaved Africans to the U.S.

During the Civil War, however, Fort Monroe **served as a refuge for those who escaped slavery.**

The walls of Fort Monroe are 10 ft (3 m) thick. Homes have walls that are only about 10 in (25 cm) thick!

ABOVE A SUNKEN MEMORY

Pearl Harbor National Memorial

Early on December 7, 1941, Japanese warplanes swarmed the U.S. naval base at Pearl Harbor. Huge bombs smashed into the USS *Arizona* and other American battleships in the harbor. During the surprise attack 1,177, sailors died on the *Arizona* alone. In total, 2,403 people were killed. The next day, the United States entered World War II (1939–1945). The memorial built over the sunken USS *Arizona* opened in 1962.

At the time, the attack on Pearl Harbor was the deadliest attack on the United States.

The USS *Arizona* before the attack

The USS *Arizona* after the attack

"Remember Pearl Harbor!" was the rallying cry for American forces during World War II.

The USS *Arizona* Memorial can only be reached by boat.

Visitors look down through an opening in the memorial's floor to see the wreck of the USS *Arizona*.

The USS *Arizona* is the final resting place for more than 900 crew members whose bodies could not be recovered from the ship.

Some survivors from the attack have chosen to have their ashes placed within the ship's wreckage after they die.

Divers place ashes into the ship during an interment ceremony.

A Monumental Craft

CRAFT PROJECT

Civil rights monuments and memorials honor the heroic efforts of those who fought for equal rights and opportunites for all. The Dr. Martin Luther King, Jr., National Memorial does just that.

Make your own monument to the civil rights movement. You can chose your favorite quote to memorialize.

The Civil Rights Memorial in Montgomery, Alabama, honors **41 people who were killed during the struggle for equality.**

What You Will Need

- A rolling pin
- Air-drying clay
- A plastic knife
- A toothpick
- Cardboard
- Glue
- Paints and brushes

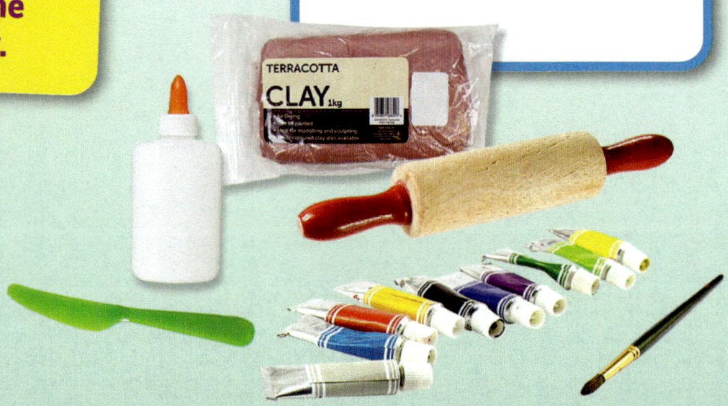

Step One

Use a rolling pin to roll clay about 0.5 in (1.3 cm) thick. Use a plastic knife to cut out a triangle shape. Roll some of the leftover clay into a ball.

Step Two

Use the toothpick to write a quote on the clay.

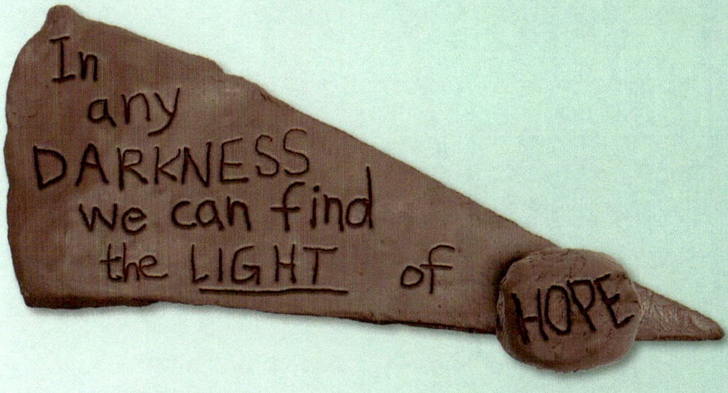

Step Three

Place the clay on your cardboard base. You might need to curve it slightly so that it stands up. Let the clay dry completely. Once it's dry, glue the sculpture to the base. Paint the base and sculpture and let it dry.

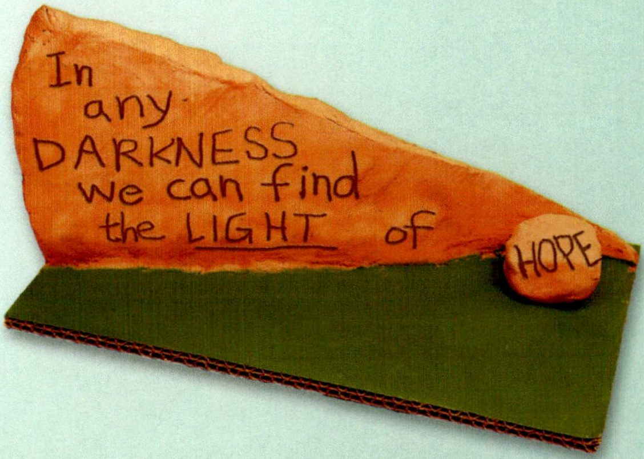

Dr. King was the youngest man to receive the Nobel Peace Prize. He was just 35 years of age.

Glossary

abandoned left empty or unused

abolitionist a person who wants to end slavery

boycott to refuse to do something as a way of forcing change

commemorate to do something special to honor or remember a person or event from the past

confederate relating to the Confederate States of America; the Confederate States of America was a group of 11 states that separated from the United States in 1860

descendants people who come from humans that lived in an earlier time

erosion the wearing away of rocks and soil by natural forces like water and wind

eruption the explosion of a volcano, or anything that appears suddenly and violently

fragile easily broken or damaged

immigrants people who come to live in a country from a different one

interment the act of putting remains or ashes in a final resting place

magma molten rock material inside Earth

mortar a soft building material that is spread between bricks or stones and holds them together when it hardens

refuge a place that gives shelter or protection

sedimentary rock formed in nature by the layering of plant and mineral material

suffrage the right to vote

symbol something that stands for something else

veterans former members of the military

Read More

Eggers, Dave. *Her Right Foot*. San Francisco, CA: Chronicle Books (2017).

Kelley, True. *Where Is Mount Rushmore?* New York: Grosset & Dunlap (2015).

McNeilly, Linden. *Historic Monuments (States Guides)*. Vero Beach, FL: Rourke Educational Media (2017).

Learn More Online

1. Go to **www.factsurfer.com**
2. Enter "**Monuments Memorials**" into the search box.
3. Click on the cover of this book to see a list of websites.

Index

About the Author

Marcia Abramson is an editor and writer in Ann Arbor, Michigan. She lives near the University of Michigan, which has lots of monuments and memorials of its own!